MIDLAND
RAILWAY
STATIONS

Allen Jackson

AMBERLEY

For Ninette.

First published 2018

Amberley Publishing
The Hill, Stroud,
Gloucestershire, GL5 4EP

www.amberley-books.com

ISBN: 978 1 4456 8043 9 (print)
ISBN: 978 1 4456 8044 6 (ebook)

British Library Cataloguing in Publication Data.
A catalogue record for this book is available from the British Library.

Typeset in 10pt on 13pt Celeste.
Origination by Amberley Publishing.
Printed in the UK.

Contents

Introduction

The Midland Railway accrued its vast wealth through coal, and while bank interest rates were paying about 3 per cent the Midland Railway was paying double that on its shares.

This enabled the railway to expand into parts of Britain that were anything but Midland, with tracks in Gloucestershire, South Wales and East Anglia together with a joint line to Bournemouth and an excursion to the border with Scotland.

In its participation with the Cheshire Lines Committee it penetrated London & North Western territory in Lancashire and North Wales.

Perhaps the most iconic route of the Midland Railway, which is the most popular and least subject to modernisation, is the Settle and Carlisle line, which was reprieved from closure by the then minister, Michael Portillo. The Ribblehead Viaduct was in need of repair and the British Railways Board put this forward as a reason for closure in the 1980s.

The line has only recently been restored to health after a disastrous landslip that severed the route.

The centre of Midland Railway operations was Derby and to this day much of the technical expertise of Network Rail is still centred in the city, although hardly anything of the station has persisted there.

In this book the contemporary Midland Railway scene is portrayed; a scene that has survived the depredations and closures of nationalisation and further modernisation in an exhaustive survey of surviving Midland Railway stations and infrastructure on Network Rail.

The preservation scene has not been included except where a heritage concern interfaces with Network Rail, such as at Keighley.

The book is arranged in terms of journeys and diagrams of the routes are included. The journeys start off at the quietest of stations by the Scottish border and end up at the teeming metropolis that is London with a postscript of Cheltenham.

Listed Buildings

Many Midland Railway structures are considered to have architectural and historic merit and are either Grade I or Grade II listed by Historic England. This means that they cannot be changed without permission. A Grade I listing would require the interiors to remain as built and some buildings have qualified, notably at St Pancras station and hotel.

Imperial and Metric Units

In the book the system of units used is the imperial system, which is what the railways themselves still use.

1 mile = 1.6 km, 1 yard = 0.92 m, 1 chain = 73.6 m. 1 chain = 22 yards. 1 mile = 1,760 yards or 80 chains.

Summary of Contents

Some stations' names have been modified in recent years, usually by being shortened, but the older names have been used to distinguish them in a pre-grouping context from other company's stations. Only those stations on the network with significant Midland Railway features are included.

SETTLE TO CARLISLE INCLUDING CLAPHAM
Cumwhinton
Armathwaite
Lazonby & Kirkoswald
Langwathby
Culgaith
Appleby
Kirkby Stephen
Garsdale (Hawes Junction)
Dent
Ribblehead
Horton-in-Ribblesdale
Settle
Clapham

WEST AND NORTH YORKSHIRE
Hellifield
Gargrave
Skipton
Keighley
Bingley
Shipley
Baildon
Menston
Ilkley

MANCHESTER TO SHEFFIELD AND DERBYSHIRE
Romiley
New Mills Central
Edale
Grindleford
Dore and Totley
Sheffield Midland
Cromford
Matlock Bath
Matlock

NOTTINGHAMSHIRE, DERBYSHIRE AND LINCOLNSHIRE
Shirebrook
Mansfield Woodhouse
Mansfield
Long Eaton
Beeston
Nottingham Midland
Lowdham
Thurgarton
Newark Castle
Collingham
Swinderby

LEICESTERSHIRE, RUTLAND, LINCOLNSHIRE, NORTHAMPTONSHIRE, BEDFORDSHIRE AND LONDON
Loughborough
Melton Mowbray
Oakham
Stamford
Leicester Midland
Market Harborough
Kettering
Wellingborough
Flitwick
Luton Leagrave
St Pancras

GLOUCESTERSHIRE
Cheltenham Spa

Midland Railway Stations

Settle to Carlisle

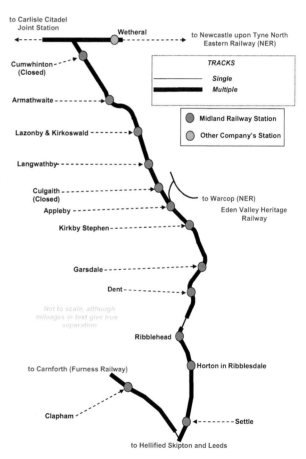

Figure 1. The journey starts near Carlisle just by the Scottish border as the intention is to show the contrast between northern and southern England in terms of railway heritage. The Midland Railway was a latecomer to the area and so had to share the way in to Carlisle with the North Eastern Railway and the two concerns were to access each other down the route. The state of Ribblehead Viaduct meant that traffic was reduced to single track over it. An interloper to the Settle and Carlisle is Clapham, which is on the original MR line to Morecambe but which now joins up with Carnforth on the West Coast Main Line and the former Furness Railway on the Cumbrian coast.

The journey heads from north to south.

Cumwhinton

Date Built	Railway/Design	Platforms	Passengers 2014–2015	Listed
1875	MR	2	Closed 1956	Grade II

Cumwhinton station closed many years ago but sympathetic owners retain the Midland Railway look, as they do all along the line on closed but inhabited stations.

Cumwhinton station is 304 miles and 12 chains (489 km) from St Pancras via Cudworth near Barnsley and Keighley.

Figure 2. The buildings are in the 'Derby Gothic' style typical of the S&C. November 2006.

Armathwaite

Date Built	Railway/Design	Platforms	Passengers 2016–2017	Listed
May 1876	MR	2	2,190	No
	Closed 1970		Reopened 1986	

Passenger numbers have more than halved since the landslip. Armathwaite was the terminus from January 2017 until March 2017, from whence a bus service operated to Carlisle.

Armathwaite station is 298 miles and 9 chains (480 km) from St Pancras via Cudworth and Keighley.

Figure 3. A general view of Armathwaite; at the far end, the goods shed and preserved signal box have survived. August 2017.

Figure 4. The station building is remarkably original and well preserved as a home. Note the gradient post on the platform; Armathwaite would appear to be a plateau. August 2017.

Figure 5. The platform waiting room at Armathwaite would usually be opened up for passengers during the day. Volunteers often produce the floral displays. August 2017.

Figure 6. The goods shed at Armathwaite has made someone a comfortable home but retains the red and white chequer plates that warn of limited clearance when shunting wagons into the shed. August 2017.

Figure 7. The signal box has no signals to control but keeps its coal bunker and lamp hut to refill long gone oil lamps. The Friends of the Settle to Carlisle Line have restored the signal box and have done much to preserve and enhance the line. August 2017.

Lazonby & Kirkoswald

Date Built	Railway/Design	Platforms	Passengers 2016–2017	Listed
May 1876	MR Closed 1970	2	4,150 Reopened 1986	No

Figure 8. The Midland Railway architect John Holloway Sanders designed Lazonby & Kirkoswald station with permanence in mind, and so it has proved. In addition to the goods shed there is also a Midland Hotel, built by the company. August 2017.

Figure 9.
Lazonby &
Kirkoswald
station waiting
room, with MR
replica diagonal
paling fencing,
is open for
passengers.
August 2017.

Figure 10.
Lazonby &
Kirkoswald
station has MR
replica diagonal
woodwork
on the doors
and cast iron
finery on the
windows. The
goods shed is in
use by a bakery.
August 2017.

Figure 11.
Lazonby &
Kirkoswald
station was
provided
with this
house for the
stationmaster.
August 2017.

Langwathby

Date Built	Railway/Design	Platforms	Passengers 2016–2017	Listed
May 1876	MR Closed 1970	2	4,132 Reopened 1986	No

Figure 12. Langwathby station with its wooden waiting shelter and goods shed. The previously high, pre-landslip passenger numbers are thought to be due to its proximity to Penrith. August 2017.

Figure 13. The station café had closed at the survey date but was due to re-open with new owners in October 2017. August 2017.

Figure 14. Although the café had closed at Langwathby, the crows don't seem to agree. The goods shed is in other use. August 2017.

Figure 15. The waiting shelter at Langwathby is, unusually for the S&C, in timber, but the MR window style remains. August 2017.

Langwathby station is 288 miles and 23 chains (464 km) from St Pancras via Cudworth and Keighley.

Culgaith

Date Built	Railway/Design	Platforms	Passengers 2016–2017	Listed
May 1880	MR Closed 1970	1	Closed	No

Figure 16. There is a mixture of semaphore and colour light signals here. August 2017.

Figure 17. The station building at Culgaith was also designed by the house architect, John Holloway Sanders, but as this was later the style is different. The view is towards Carlisle and just beyond the tunnel was the scene of an incident where a train ignored a signal and crashed into a ballast train in 1930. August 2017.

Figure 18. The way south towards Appleby and Settle is guarded by the colour light signal at Culgaith, while the loading gauge frame from another era looks on. August 2017.

Culgaith signal box is 284 miles and 55 chains (458 km) from St Pancras via Cudworth and Keighley.

Appleby

Date Built	Railway/Design	Platforms	Passengers 2016–2017	Listed
May 1876	MR	2	88,936	Grade II

The passenger figures are about 25,000 higher than normal because of a change of working due to the landslip.

Appleby station is 277 miles and 22 chains (446 km) from St Pancras via Cudworth and Keighley.

Figure 19. Appleby station has many MR features as well as a Midland Hotel outside the station. August 2017.

Figure 20. Appleby station has a cosy waiting room, toilets and buffet, and is also the replenishment point for the on-train trolley services operated for Northern Rail. It also has a plaque commemorating the noted railway photographer Eric Treacy, the Bishop of Wakefield, who died on Appleby station. August 2017.

Figure 21. The waiting room at Appleby has authentic-looking platform seats outside. Note also the fire bucket bracket at the end, by the diagonally timbered door. August 2017.

Figure 22. At the end of the same platform at Appleby is this MR water column and tower. August 2017.

Figure 23. Looking north at Appleby is the ex-LMS signal box and the junction for a few sidings and to the line to Warcop, which is ex-NER. The North Eastern Railway had their own station at Appleby at the Grouping in 1923, and a line to Penrith. August 2017.

Figure 24. The view south to Kirkby Stephen from Appleby shows the goods shed, which is now the home of Appleby Training and Heritage Centre, which conducts training in a large range of disciplines. The covered wagon on the extreme right is a restored salt wagon. August 2017.

Figure 25. Finally, at Appleby the name 'APPLEBY' is depicted in whitewashed stones. It was a common practice in days gone by and was put together by station staff, who regarded those sorts of gardening duties as part of the job. Appleby received an award in 2003 as the best small station. August 2017.

Kirkby Stephen

Date Built	Railway/Design	Platforms	Passengers 2016–2017	Listed
1876	MR Closed 1970	2	19,982 Reopened 1986	No (O'bridge Y)

Figure 26. Kirkby Stephen station was restored by the S&C Railway Trust in 2005 and the waiting shelter looks to be from about that date, although it is in keeping with the MR ethos and ideals. The station is some 1½ miles (2.4 km) from the town and this is like Appleby in that the NER had a station here too, the difference being that the NER station survives as Kirkby Stephen East under the care of a heritage group, the Stainmore Railway Company. October 2014.

Figure 27. Northern Rail Class 158 No. 158848 heads for Leeds and makes up one of the seven weekday trains. There are two self-catering cottages for rent on the platform. August 2017.

Figure 28. The station building at Kirkby Stephen makes a pair of admirable holiday homes with the un-MR-like attribute of WiFi. August 2017.

Figure 29. The view towards Leeds reveals the footbridge, LMR signal box, goods shed and moorland scenery. There are two refuge sidings to hold trains in difficulty. August 2003.

Figure 30. The goods shed looks to be heading for its 150th anniversary with confidence, but the 1950s BR signal box less so. The goods shed keeps its 'Warning Limited Clearance' enamel plates by the wagon entrance door. August 2017.

Kirkby Stephen station is 266 miles and 47 chains (429 km) from St Pancras via Cudworth and Keighley.

Garsdale

Date Built	Railway/Design	Platforms	Passengers 2016–2017	Listed
1876	MR Closed 1970	2	12,520 Reopened 1986	No (S'Box Y)

The station had been the junction for the branch to Hawes, which formed an end-on junction with the NER, which the heritage Wensleydale Railway is keen to restore.

Garsdale station is 256 miles and 53 chains (413 km) from St Pancras via Cudworth and Keighley.

Figure 31. A general view of Garsdale, looking north towards Carlisle, and the line curves around to the left over Dandry Mire or Mooorcock Viaduct. On view is the steam-age water tower, station buildings, railway workers' cottages and signal box, but there is no goods shed here. John Holloway Sanders was the architect once again but the buildings are simpler than at other stations. July 2003.

Figure 32. A Garsdale signaller was responsible for a collision near here in 1910 when an express passenger train ran into the back of a pair of light engines that were returning over Ais Gill summit to Carlisle. July 2003.

Figure 33. The minimal station building at Garsdale is unusual on the S&C. The restored 'TRAINS TO CARLISLE' board is echoed with 'LEEDS' on the other platform. Both tracks expect a train soon and at the time the route was in use for freight trains avoiding the WCML. July 2003.

Figure 34. At the end of the platforms at Garsdale, looking towards Carlisle, is the site of some of the Hawes branch trackwork over by the ballast pile and sleepers. The trailing crossover allows either track to access the refuge sidings. July 2003.

Dent

Date Built	Railway/Design	Platforms	Passengers 2016–2017	Listed
August 1877	MR Closed 1970	2	7,248 Reopened 1986	Grade II

Figure 35. Dent station is on a sharp curve and the signal box was behind the camera on the apex of the curve. The whitewashed area of the bridge ahead acted as a sighting board for one of the box's signals. The view is north to Garsdale and Carlisle. November 2006.

Figure 36. The building after the station is part of the workers' barracks, which, as well as the station, are also listed. November 2006.

Figure 37. The quality and realism of the restoration of the main building is evident in this view, which now shows the station fenced off from its platform. November 2006.

Figure 38. Dent is now the highest station in England. The snow fence behind the railway fence is partly made of old sleepers. November 2006.

Dent station is 253 miles and 32 chains (408 km) from St Pancras via Cudworth and Keighley.

Ribblehead

Date Built	Railway/Design	Platforms	Passengers 2016–2017	Listed
1876	MR Closed 1970	2	17,734 Reopened 1986	No

Figure 39. Ribblehead station reverts to the more usual Settle and Carlisle architecture after the 'lite' approach at Garsdale, although the same architect was employed on both. The staggered platform in the distance is a comparatively recent innovation as the original second platform was demolished after closure in 1970. The view is looking south towards Settle and Leeds. November 2006.

Figure 40. Although Ribblehead station is not listed, it has been magnificently restored and now has a visitor information centre, shop and small museum. The nearby Ribblehead barracks construction camp under the viaduct is Grade II listed. November 2006.

Figure 41. The waiting room sits on the 1993 constructed platform. The platform had been demolished to make way for sidings connected with quarry traffic and now, added to that, is cut timber for the Kronospan chipboard works at Chirk. November 2006.

Figure 42. Low cloud and mist shroud the hills as the line heads north, briefly as single track, over Ribblehead or Batty Moss Viaduct, then on to Blea Moor signal box and Dent. Opposite the station building is a ground frame for changing the siding points, but the rest of the layout is controlled by Blea Moor. November 2006.

Ribblehead station Down platform is 247 miles and 13 chains (397.77 km) and the Up platform towards Leeds is 247 miles and 20 chains (397.91 km) from St Pancras via Cudworth and Keighley.

Horton-in-Ribblesdale

Date Built	Railway/Design	Platforms	Passengers 2016–2017	Listed
1876	MR Closed 1970	2	16,112 Reopened 1986	No

Figure 43. Horton-in-Ribblesdale station is perched on a ledge above the village so there is no expansive area behind the station building. The lamp hut survives but the signal box does not. February 2018.

Figure 44. Horton-in-Ribblesdale station building's conservation standards are as high as any on the line, with extraordinarily detailed window frames. February 2018.

Figure 45. The opposite platform at Horton-in-Ribblesdale is just as cramped as the other side. This is a colour light signal area. February 2018.

Figure 46. The altitude the station is at is not particularly fearsome, but combined with the latitude it can be a cold place. Note the stationmaster's house behind. February 2018.

Horton in Ribblesdale station is 242 miles and 43 chains (390 km) from St Pancras via Cudworth and Keighley.

Settle

Date Built	Railway/Design	Platforms	Passengers 2016–2017	Listed
1876	MR	2	0.12 million	Grade II

Settle station is a hub for walkers, hikers and visitors to the area and has a museum dedicated to the Midland Railway.

Settle station is 236 miles and 40 chains (381 km) from St Pancras via Cudworth and Keighley.

Figure 47. At Settle station the main building has an extra wing on each side and the stationmaster's house is on the platform so that he can be on the job. Note the extremely large water tower in the background, which would have fed columns for the locomotives. February 2018.

Figure 48. The footbridge is an interloper from the North British Railway station at Drem on the ECML, but looks tolerably Midland Railway-like. February 2018.

Figure 49. Settle station is very much a showplace in summer and the converted porter's trolley does second duty as a planter. July 2003.

Figure 50. Preserved as part of the Midland Railway exhibition is this MR signal box and home and distant signal; there is also another home signal behind the box. Originally the MR had lower quadrant signals. Note the lamp hut and water column. February 2018.

Figure 51. Just by the station yard is this exhibition of Midland Railwayana, plus a private owner wagon from a local company. February 2018.

Figure 52. A couple of miles from Settle station is Settle Junction, where the MR signal box controls the points and signals for the S&C's junction with the Morecambe (NWR) line, which is on the far right of the picture. Freightliner Class 66 No. 66515 wheels a train of coal empties on their way back to Hunterston in Ayrshire. October 2014.

There is now a brief excursion up the branch line towards Carnforth that had originally been part of the Leeds to Morecambe line on the Midland Railway, with a connection with the WCML at Lancaster Green Ayre station. The line was known as the 'Little North Western Railway' after the founding company (NWR) and it was as close as the MR got to invading the 'Premier Line's' territory in the North West with the possible exception of the joint Cheshire Lines Committee (CLC).

Clapham

Date Built	Railway/Design	Platforms	Passengers 2016–2017	Listed
1849	North Western Railway	2	7,248	Grade II MR Bldg, 1870

Clapham station is described by Historic England as 'Clapham-cum-Newby' station.

The mileages are calculated from the same route as the S&C and Clapham station is 242 miles and 0 chains (389 km) from St Pancras via Cudworth and Keighley.

Figure 53. Clapham station had a branch line hereabouts, and so was Clapham Junction for a time. Now it is very quiet on the NWR to Morecambe. February 2018.

West Yorkshire

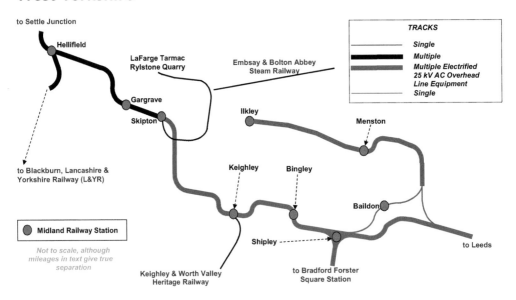

Figure 54.

Hellifield is the last of the old-school Midland Railway installations, complete with semaphore signalling, and Skipton sees the start of the intensive electrified services around Leeds and Bradford. The route continues across the county heading east with a branch line to Ilkley, which then doubles back to the west. There are two heritage lines, which both have a Midland Railway history.

Hellifield

Date Built	Railway/Design	Platforms	Passengers 2016–2017	Listed
circa 1880	Midland Railway (Original site 1849)	2 (4 Faces)	29,916	Grade II

Hellifield is a unique Midland Railway design and is the junction with the former Lancashire & Yorkshire Railway line to the cotton towns of Lancashire.

Hellifield station is 231 miles and 20 chains (372 km) from St Pancras via Cudworth and Keighley.

Figure 55. Hellifield station is near the junction with the Lancashire & Yorkshire line to Blackburn and so importantly has an individually designed set of platform canopies quite unlike any other that survive. March 2007.

Figure 56. Inside the canopies at Hellifield the MR logo and the company's griffin is cast into the ironwork. Each canopy extends for some way on one side only, but at opposite sides, so there is an equal covered area for each main platform but asymmetrically disposed. February 2018.

Figure 57. This image illustrates one end of the asymmetric canopy and the bay platform here is fenced off. This is the side the subway emerges from. March 2007.

Figure 58. The opposite end reveals the remnants of the buffer stops of the bay platform that faces north. The kiosk at the end of the building looks like a newsstand. February 2018.

Figure 59. Northern Rail Class 142 No. 142079 heads north from Hellifield station with an endurance trip to Morecambe. The signal the set is passing is for the next-door track. February 2018.

Figure 60. The rear of the Midland Railway signal box at Hellifield South Junction is to include a semaphore signal gantry at the south end of the station and the actual junction with the former L&Y line. March 2007.

Gargrave

Date Built	Railway/Design	Platforms	Passengers 2016–2017	Listed
1849	North Western Railway then MR	2	27,856	No

Gargrave station is 224 miles and 79 chains (362 km) from St Pancras via Cudworth and Keighley.

Figure 61. Gargrave station has an unusual mixture of styles, with a half-timbered look for the main station building and stone for the waiting shelter on the opposite platform. October 2017.

Figure 62. Gargrave waiting shelter is a survivor. It has intricate cast iron window frames – an MR trademark. October 2017.

Skipton

Date Built	Railway/Design	Platforms	Passengers 2016–2017	Listed
1876 (This site)	Midland Railway	4	1.138 million	Grade II

Skipton station is 221 miles and 21 chains (356 km) from St Pancras via Cudworth and Keighley.

Figure 63. This is the second station built at Skipton and, designed by Charles Trubshaw, coincided with the opening of the Settle and Carlisle line in 1876. The building style is restrained and comfortable rather than majestic or grandiose. October 2017.

Figure 64. For the first time we see another Midland Railway station trademark, that of the saw-toothed platform canopy with its attendant cast iron finery and a finial on every tooth tip. The camera is on the island platform, which comprises Platforms 3 and 4, and is looking across to the main platform, Platform 2. October 2017.

Figure 65. The station was built up to have six platforms but the branches to Grassington and Ilkley from Skipton closed; however, Platform 5 survives unused on the extreme left out of shot. The bay Platform 1 is on the extreme right. October 2017.

Figure 66. Class 150 Sprinter No. 150123 has arrived at Platform 2 at Skipton with a diesel train from Carlisle bound for Leeds. October 2017.

Keighley

Date Built	Railway/Design	Platforms	Passengers 2016–2017	Listed
1885 (This site)	Midland Railway	4 (includes K&WVR)	1.705 million	Grade II

The station is shared with the Keighley & Worth Valley Heritage Railway.

Keighley station is 212 miles and 6 chains (341 km) from St Pancras via Cudworth.

Figure 67. The Midland Railway griffins are in evidence on the faintly saw-toothed canopy at Keighley, and as another junction, this station has presence. October 2017.

Figure 68. The station has two parts: the Network Rail part shown here and the K&WVR part. Historic England was not as complimentary about this part as the other. October 2017.

Figure 69. The Network Rail waiting room is tolerably original and has a modern kiosk. October 2017.

Figure 70. The division of NR to the left and K&WVR to the right is evident here. The throngs of mill workers can easily be imagined here. October 2017.

Figure 71. The K&WVR platforms are as if in a 1950s/60s time warp and are frequently used by film companies. The waiting room atrium is on the main building skyline. West Coast Railways had sent the ex-LMS Black 5 4-6-0 locomotive No. 44871 and support coach here for a test run prior to employment. October 2017.

Figure 72. The ramp down to the platform that we saw in Figure 70 is clearly on show here as well as the K&WVR bookstall and other heritage items. There is a large water tower and signal box here that are part of the listing as well as a turntable, water column and other artefacts. August 2007.

Bingley

Date Built	Railway/Design	Platforms	Passengers 2016–2017	Listed
1892 (This site)	Midland Railway	2	1.255 million	No

While there are properties in Station Road that are listed, the station itself has been overlooked.

Bingley station is 208 miles and 68 chains (336 km) from St Pancras via Cudworth.

Figure 73. Bingley station main building has two engraved stones beneath the finial balls on the gable ends. The nearer says 'MR' and the further '1892'. February 2018.

Figure 74. Platform 2 at Bingley station sees the departure of Metro Class 333 No. 333015 on a service to Bradford Forster Square. This is one of ninety-six such weekdaily workings. February 2018.

Figure 75. The saw-toothed canopy on Platform 1 at Bingley appears to be cut down to a minimum. February 2018.

Shipley

Date Built	Railway/Design	Platforms	Passengers 2016–2017	Listed
Circa 1892 (This site)	Midland Railway	5 (6 Faces)	1.745 million	No

Shipley station is 205 miles and 72 chains (331 km) from St Pancras via Cudworth.

Figure 76. Triple junctions on overground trains are rare in Britain but Shipley has five platforms and some surviving MR buildings from the complex. The booking hall is on the extreme left. October 2017.

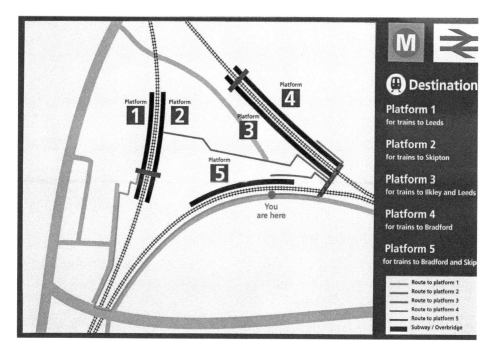

Figure 77. The West Yorkshire Metro board explains the platforms and their uses very well. When looking at Figure 79 you need to rotate the diagram by 90 degrees clockwise to get a sense of the layout. October 2017.

Figure 78. Platform 5 at Shipley and clearly there had been a Platform 6 in the foreground. This would have serviced Down trains to Skipton and Platform 5 Up trains from Skipton. The line was converted to single track just here so Platform 5 now serves both Down and Up. October 2017.

Figure 79. Platform 3 retains an MR flavour, whereas much else in the station at Shipley has been modernised. Platform 5 is off to the left. October 2017.

Baildon

Date Built	Railway/Design	Platforms	Passengers 2016–2017	Listed
1876	Midland Railway	1 (2 faces)	0.290 million	No

Figure 80. Baildon station is reduced to one platform and the station building is now a tyre depot. Class 333 No. 333001 calls on its way to Shipley and Bradford Forster Square. February 2018.

Baildon station is 2 miles and 29 chains (356 km) from Esholt Junction, near Guiseley.

Menston

Date Built	Railway/Design	Platforms	Passengers 2016–2017	Listed
1865	Midland Railway	2	0.667 million	No

Menston station building has a smart ticket office, which is open office hours, and the premises are shared with a local nursery.

Menston station is 206 miles and 53 chains (333 km) from St Pancras via Cudworth.

Figure 81. The upmarket Menston station building is quite substantial for a suburban station. February 2018.

Figure 82. Even the waiting room on the opposite platform at Menston has MR presence. Up until 1965, trains to Otley could be caught here. February 2018.

Ilkley

Date Built	Railway/Design	Platforms	Passengers 2016–2017	Listed
1865	Midland Railway	2 (were 4)	1.358 million	Grade II

Ilkley has adapted to its reduced size but is still busy and prosperous. Although Ilkley is forever associated with the moors, it is 1 foot (305 mm) lower in altitude than Bradford Forster Square station.

Ilkley station is 211 miles and 20 chains (340 km) from St Pancras via Cudworth.

Figure 83. The original booking hall and waiting rooms at Ilkley have been given over to lucrative retail outlets to woo the Bradford or Leeds-bound commuters. September 2018.

Figure 84. The station had originally been four platforms and the saw-toothed canopies in what is now the car park are evidence of this. Electric multiple unit Class 333 No. 333008 forms the 12.51 service to Bradford Forster Square. September 2018.

Manchester to Sheffield and Derbyshire

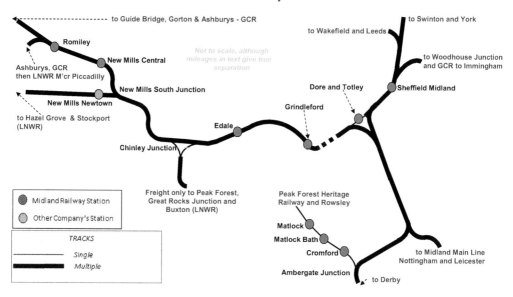

Figure 85. Manchester to Sheffield.

The simplified diagram at Figure 85 gives some idea of the complexity of lines in the area and around Peak Forest of the Midland Main line to Manchester Central until 1968, although Peak Rail have ambitions to restore some of the closures. The small town of New Mills had three railway stations of LNWR, Midland and Midland and GC Joint Railway ownership. Only the first and last survive but it gives some idea of the complexity and competition for traffic there was. The journey begins in the Stockport suburb of Romiley and ends up at the iconic spa town of Matlock.

Romiley

Date Built	Railway/Design	Platforms	Passengers 2016–2017	Listed
1862	MS&LR & Midland Railway	2	0.359 million	No

The blue plaque outside the building states that the building was built by the Manchester, Sheffield & Lincolnshire Railway, a forerunner of the GCR, but there are MR features, such as diagonal braced doors as well as an MR signal box, which is now closed.

Romiley station is 178 miles and 27 chains (287 km) from St Pancras via Millers Dale.

Figure 86. Romiley is a joint station with the Great Central Railway and is also a junction, so was seen to be of some importance when it was built. The height of the building is to enable street level to connect with the elevated railway above Stockport Road. January 2018.

Figure 87. Class 150 No. 150220 comes off the branch from Manchester Piccadilly, past the now closed MR signal box, to arrive at the Up platform at Romiley with a Sheffield service. Another train is signalled for the Down platform for Piccadilly. January 2018.

Figure 88. The Up platform at Romiley towards Sheffield. The entrance doorway leads to the subway. January 2018.

Date Built	Railway/Design	Platforms	Passengers 2016–2017	Listed
1865	MS&LR & Midland Railway	2	0.209 million	No

Another joint station that had a GCR line running parallel to the present one and the tunnel mouth for the GC line is still visible. The signal box here is active at the survey date.

New Mills Central station is 173 miles and 15 chains (279 km) from St Pancras via Millers Dale.

Figure 89. New Mills Central station is dominated by the stationmaster's house on the end. The MR footbridge provides a frame for the MR signal box, which is still in use. January 2018.

Figure 90. The road overbridge provides the rostrum for this view of New Mills Central towards Manchester. Just past the Up platform on the right is a turn back siding to enable a DMU that terminates here to regain the correct running line. The station is built on a ledge above the River Goyt. January 2018.

Edale

Date Built	Railway/Design	Platforms	Passengers 2016–2017	Listed
1894	Midland Railway	2	89,510	No

Into the Hope Valley proper and the original timber buildings have been demolished, but there is a signal box, bridges and an underpass that are pure MR.

Edale station is 169 miles and 14 chains (272 km) from St Pancras via Toton and Chesterfield.

Figure 91. The Up platform at Edale provides this view of a DMU stopped in section and the severed goods refuge sidings, which don't seem long enough for modern freight trains. January 2018.

Grindleford

Date Built	Railway/Design	Platforms	Passengers 2016–2017	Listed
1894	Midland Railway	2	66,442	No

The station building is situated on the road that crosses the railway and is now a café popular with walkers and hikers.

Grindleford station is 159 miles and 6 chains (256 km) from St Pancras via Toton and Chesterfield.

Figure 92. The station building café at Grindleford serves tea in mugs and no-nonsense food, and is often packed at weekends. January 2018.

Figure 93. Travelling towards Sheffield light engine, Freightliner Class 66 No. 66605 leans into the curve at the Up platform at Grindleford. The signal on the opposite platform is off for a trans-Pennine DMU. January 2018.

Figure 94. Looking the other way from the previous figure at Grindleford and the signal is off for the Class 66. The road overbridge where the station building is provides a whitewashed sighting board for the signal and Totley Tunnel, behind the bridge, is 3 miles and 950 yards (5.7 km) long. The inscription reads '1893 Totley Tunnel' and below that, out of shot, is an MR logo carved in stone. January 2018.

Dore and Totley

Date Built	Railway/Design	Platforms	Passengers 2016–2017	Listed
1872	Midland Railway	1	0.165 million	No

Out of the other side of Totley Tunnel now, into Yorkshire, and Dore and Totley had been a considerable junction station with the Midland Railway main line up until the 1960s.

Dore and Totley station is 154 miles and 19 chains (248 km) from St Pancras via Toton and Leicester.

Figure 95. Dore station serves duty as a restaurant now and commuters wait for their early morning train to Sheffield Midland on the single platform. The double track to the Midland main line is on the right. February 2018.

Sheffield Midland

Date Built	Railway/Design	Platforms	Passengers 2016–2017	Listed
1904 remodelled	Midland Railway Charles Trubshaw	9	10.592 million	Grade II

Sheffield Midland, as opposed to Victoria, the LNER Great Central station, is now known as just Sheffield.

Sheffield Midland station is 158 miles and 40 chains (255 km) from St Pancras via Toton and Leicester.

Figure 96. Sheffield Midland was originally called Pond Street with an older building, but the later effort by Charles Trubshaw was the largest MR station after St Pancras. The arcaded porte-cochère would have seen hansom cabs as well as early motor cars when first built. February 2018.

Figure 97. Sheffield Midland and through the porte-cochère is this elegant circulating area, which is now mostly full of retail outlets. February 2018.

Figure 98. The main buildings at Sheffield Midland, across the tracks in this view, have distinctive chimney stacks. After the main platform, which has a Pacer Class 142 standing at it, is an island that has three bay platforms, one of which contains the Class 150 DMU. After the island, coming towards the camera, is a further island platform with one bay but which has been modernised. February 2018.

Figure 99. Sheffield Midland station at the southern end with a DMU in the first island bay and plenty of MR buildings, but not as ornate as the main ones. On the near side of the near island are the Sheffield Supertram tracks. February 2018.

Figure 100. Sheffield Midland, looking north to the Granville Street overbridge, but the bridge is more complicated as there is a retaining wall built in that is holding back part of the Pennines. The through tracks remain where a lot of stations have seen them removed after the reduction in through freight traffic. February 2018.

Figure 101. Sheffield Midland, with the main platform and buildings on the left and the first island on the right, both with lots of MR character. February 2018.

There is now a short excursion down what is today marketed as the Derwent Valley Line.

Cromford

Date Built	Railway/Design	Platforms	Passengers 2016–2017	Listed
1849	Midland Railway G. H. Stokes	1 (2 Faces)	47,400	Grade II

Cromford is principally known for its historical connection with Richard Arkwright, and the nearby Cromford Mill and canal. The area is in the Derwent Valley World Heritage site.

Cromford station is 143 miles and 10 chains (230 km) from St Pancras via Leicester and Chaddesdon.

Figure 102. Cromford station, looking north towards Manchester. This is an unlikely celebration in stone for a village wayside station, and even the stationmaster's house up on the hill is a delight. Both buildings on the right are now holiday lets. January 2018.

Figure 103. The main station building at Cromford is not in railway use any longer and the taller building at the end looks as though it had been a signal box. January 2018.

Figure 104. Even though the station building at Cromford does not belong to a railway company, it still affords accommodation for East Midlands Trains' passengers, one of whom will shortly board an EMT Class 153 single-car DMU. January 2018.

Figure 105. A fine waiting room at a country station, which won an award for its restoration. January 2018.

Matlock Bath

Date Built	Railway/Design	Platforms	Passengers 2016–2017	Listed
1849	Midland Railway (forerunner of)	1 (was 2)	75,608 Closed 1967	Grade II Reopened 1972

Matlock and the surrounding area were promoted by the Midland Railway to be the Switzerland of England, hence the alpine chalet style architecture.

Matlock Bath station is 143 miles and 73 chains (232 km) from St Pancras via Leicester and Chaddesdon.

Figure 106. The Midland Railway promoted the Derbyshire Peak District as Little Switzerland and this example of a Swiss chalet type of station building at Matlock Bath is extraordinary. January 2018.

Figure 107. Also on the platform is a further building towards the north end of the station and this too is listed. It is now difficult to imagine that this was a double tracked main line. January 2018.

Figure 108. On the platform at Matlock Bath and the incredible complexity of the brickwork is complemented by typically ornate MR cast iron window frames and diagonally timber-braced doors. January 2018.

Matlock

Date Built	Railway/Design	Platforms	Passengers 2016–2017	Listed
1849	Midland Railway (forerunner of)	2 (shared)	0.222 million (Network Rail)	No

Matlock is currently the terminus of the Derwent Valley Line and the station is shared with the Peak Rail heritage railway. Although the station is not listed, the stationmaster's house is.

Matlock station is 145 miles (233 km) from St Pancras via Leicester and Chaddesdon.

Figure 109. Matlock's Network Rail service platform is the far one and the near is Peak Rail's, which ends in buffer stops before Boathouse Bridge, where the camera is. The second smaller station building on the Network Rail platform looks likely to have been added in 1875, when the footbridge and buildings on what is now the Peak Rail platform were added. These were subsequently demolished. January 2018.

Figure 110. Peak Rail still has a presence on the NR platform at Matlock in the shape of their shop. The stationmaster's house here is listed. January 2018.

Figure 111. At the end of Platform 1 is a run-round loop for engineer's trains and the end of the Network Rail line at Matlock and the beginning of Peak Rail's, whose platform is on the left. January 2018.

Nottinghamshire, Derbyshire and Lincolnshire

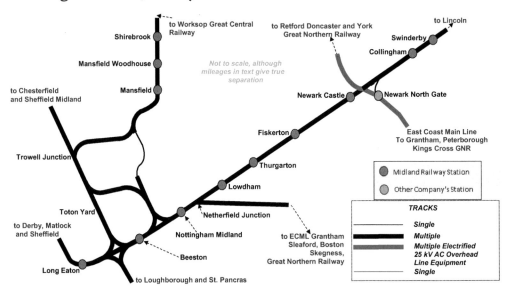

Figure 112. Nottinghamshire, Derbyshire and Lincolnshire.

The simplified diagram at Figure 112 hints at the complexity of Midland Railway infrastructure around the Nottinghamshire coalfield and the massive yards at Toton still exist, although they have been cut down in later years. The journey begins on the line from Worksop, which is now marketed as the 'Robin Hood' line, and much of it had been closed and demolished under BR. Next we visit the outskirts of Nottingham before reaching Midland station. The line from Midland station heads north-east towards Lincolnshire.

Shirebrook

Date Built	Railway/Design	Platforms	Passengers 2016–2017	Listed
1875	Midland Railway Closed 1964	2	84,848 Re-opened 1998	No

Figure 113. Shirebrook station building sees another use now. The former diesel depot is off to the left, out of shot. February 2018.

Shirebrook in Derbyshire is close to a triple junction formed by mostly colliery lines and a connection with the Great Central (LNER) at Clipstone Junction.

Shirebrook station is 145 miles and 6 chains (233 km) from St Pancras via Corby and Newstead.

Mansfield Woodhouse

Date Built	Railway/Design	Platforms	Passengers 2016–2017	Listed
1995	Midland Railway pattern, Railtrack	3	0.179 million	No

Into Nottinghamshire and the station building platform shelter has been built in the MR style and resembles a small goods shed.

Mansfield Woodhouse station is 142 miles and 17 chains (229 km) from St Pancras via Corby and Newstead.

Figure 114. Although the purpose of this book is to portray original MR structures, this modern example seems worthy of inclusion in the best traditions of the MR. February 2018.

Mansfield

Date Built	Railway/Design	Platforms	Passengers 2016–2017	Listed
1872	Midland Railway Closed 1964	2	0.399 million Re-opened 1995	Grade II

Mansfield's main station building survived closure to become listed and a Midland Hotel completes the local scene.

Mansfield station is 140 miles and 44 chains (226 km) from St Pancras via Corby and Newstead.

The journey continues from Derbyshire at Long Eaton to Nottingham and towards Lincoln.

Figure 115. The station building at Mansfield is not improved by the modern canopy. February 2018.

Figure 116. The cobbled forecourt is in keeping with the ornate decoration around the windows and doors. Increasingly ornate chimney stacks feature in MR architecture, depending on how important the station is. The Midland Hotel is off to the left and rear. February 2018.

Long Eaton

Date Built	Railway/Design	Platforms	Passengers 2016–2017	Listed
1888	Midland Railway	2	0.635 million	No

Although the station is not listed, the nearby Tamworth Road Bridge carrying the railway over the road is an early Midland Counties Railway structure, dated 1837–8 by Historic England.

Long Eaton station is 120 miles and 28 chains (194 km) from St Pancras via Leicester.

Figure 117. Despite the modern intruder defences, it is possible to see something of the half-timbered look of Clapham and Gargrave. This building is one of the few that carries out its original function at a wayside station. February 2018.

Beeston

Date Built	Railway/Design	Platforms	Passengers 2016–2017	Listed
1847	Midland Railway	2	0.399 million	Grade II

Beeston station dates from 1839 and was built for the Midland Counties Railway, but the station building is MR and dated later. The canopy on Platform 1 and the shelters on both platforms are included in the listing and date from 1871.

Beeston station is 123 miles and 22 chains (198 km) from St Pancras via Leicester and Trent.

Figure 118. The station building at Beeston is in white brick and part rendered according to Historic England. The two lozenges beneath the gables pronounce 'MR' and '1847'. The East Midland Trains DMU Class 170 No. 170105 is stopping at Platform 1 to pick up passengers for Nottingham Midland. The goods shed also survives here. February 2018.

Figure 119. Platform 2 at Beeston has the shelters, which are considered rare by Historic England. February 2018.

Nottingham Midland

Date Built	Railway/Design	Platforms	Passengers 2016–2017	Listed
1904 rebuilt	Midland Railway Albert E. Lambert & Charles Trubshaw	7	7.469 million	Grade II

Victoria, the LNER Great Central/Great Northern joint station, which is now demolished, was designed by the same architect and consequently shared some characteristics.

Nottingham Midland station is 118 miles and 40 chains (191 km) from St Pancras via Toton and Leicester.

Figure 120. The magnificently restored Nottingham Midland station is a statement from the MR at the height of its power and wealth in the Edwardian era, and the importance of Nottingham as a destination. February 2018.

Figure 121. Nottingham Midland station at the Carrington Street entrance is no less imposing and impressive with ornate stonework decoration. Historic England describe it as: 'Constructed of a mixture of red brick, terracotta and faience [glazed terracotta] with slate and glazed pitch roofs over the main buildings. Neo-Baroque style.' February 2018.

Figure 122. This view from the adjacent tram station shows the passenger concourse building on the left leading down through footbridges to the platforms. The builders are in because of the January 2018 arson attack. February 2018.

Figure 123. The opposite view to the previous from the tram station shows the station buildings on each main platform – Platforms 3 and 4 and their canopies – looking towards Lincoln. February 2018.

Figure 124. Platform 3 seen from Platform 4, depicting the left-hand side of the two in the previous figure in more detail. February 2018.

Figure 125. Platform 5 was housing this East Midlands Trains HST set, No. 43030, when photographed. The bay window belonged to Nottingham 'B' semaphore signal box, which was built with the station rebuilding in 1904. February 2018.

Figure 126. The passenger concourse at Nottingham Midland was singled out for praise by Historic England. The station cost £1 million to build in 1904. February 2018.

Lowdham

Date Built	Railway/Design	Platforms	Passengers 2016–2017	Listed
circa 1846	Midland Railway Thomas C. Hine	2	57,236	Grade II

Lowdham station building is in private hands but is maintained as a museum dedicated to the Midland Railway and its successors.

The place from which the mileage is calculated changes at Nottingham, and Lowdham station is 7 miles and 27 chains (12 km) from London Road Junction, Nottingham.

Figure 127. Lowdham station has the following exhibits in its private museum: Lowdham oil lamp, Lowdham enamel running in board, MR cast sign, fire buckets, upper quadrant semaphore signal, ventilated van body and MR bill boards. There is also a Victorian post box on the front of the building. The signal box remains but has lost its Network Rail semaphores. February 2018.

Thurgarton

Date Built	Railway/Design	Platforms	Passengers 2016–2017	Listed
1847	Midland Railway	2	2,470	Grade II

Thurgarton main station building is also the work of Thomas Chambers Hine.

Thurgarton station is 9 miles and 43 chains (15 km) from London Road Junction, Nottingham.

Figure 128. Thurgarton station has the Up platform towards Nottingham on the other side of a road crossing. February 2018.

Fiskerton

Date Built	Railway/Design	Platforms	Passengers 2016–2017	Listed
1846	Midland Railway	2	26,760	No

Fiskerton main station building has gone but the stationmaster's house remains, along with the signal box which looked after the crossing gates.

Thurgarton station is 12 miles and 46 chains (20 km) from London Road Junction, Nottingham.

Figure 129. The gate signal box at Fiskerton has had nothing to do after automatic barriers were installed. The frame remains within the box and so do the now untended window boxes, which were such a feature here. February 2018.

Newark Castle

Date Built	Railway/Design	Platforms	Passengers 2016–2017	Listed
1846	Midland Railway	2	0.752 million	Grade II

The Newark Castle main station building, stationmaster's house, signal box and goods shed all survive.

Newark Castle station is 17 miles and 3 chains (27 km) from London Road Junction, Nottingham.

Figure 130. The main station building at Newark Castle has a booking office at the near end and a café. There is no footbridge here and passengers reach the Down platform by crossing the Great North Road. The goods shed is in the distance. February 2018.

Figure 131. The signal box at Newark Castle has no semaphore signals and the crossover in the station where trains could turn back to Nottingham has been removed. The stationmaster's house is next door. February 2018.

Collingham

Date Built	Railway/Design	Platforms	Passengers 2016–2017	Listed
circa 1848	Midland Railway	2	0.103 million	Grade II

Collingham station building is quite unlike any other on the line; often, an unusual style or magnificence was at the behest of the local landowner.

Collingham station is 22 miles and 17 chains (36 km) from London Road Junction, Nottingham.

Figure 132. The two porch rooves either side of the projecting bay have suffered a bit. Historic England describes the building as being in the Italianate style. February 2018.

Swinderby

Date Built	Railway/Design	Platforms	Passengers 2016–2017	Listed
1846	Midland Railway	2	14,462	Grade II

Swinderby station building is accompanied by a waiting shelter, station house, signal box, manual crossing gates and semaphore signals.

Swinderby station is 24 miles and 64 chains (40 km) from London Road Junction, Nottingham.

Figure 133. Of the buildings in this view, only the signal box, built 1901, is not listed. The waiting shelter resembles Cromford and the view is towards Lincoln. February 2018.

Leicestershire, Rutland, Lincolnshire, Northamptonshire, Bedfordshire and London

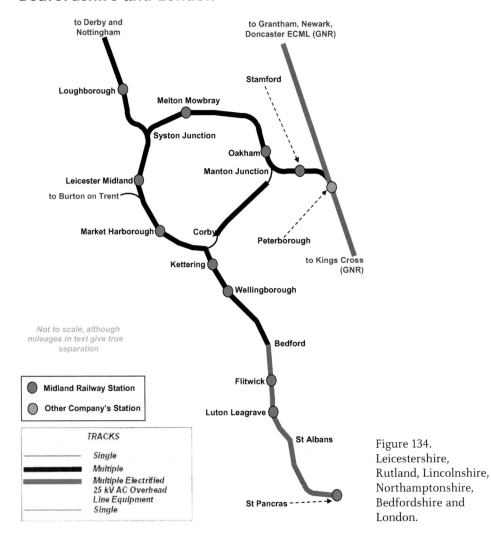

to Derby and Nottingham

to Grantham, Newark, Doncaster ECML (GNR)

Loughborough

Stamford

Melton Mowbray

Syston Junction

Oakham

Manton Junction

Leicester Midland

to Burton on Trent

Market Harborough

Corby

Peterborough

Kettering

to Kings Cross (GNR)

Wellingborough

Not to scale, although mileages in text give true separation

Bedford

Flitwick

● Midland Railway Station

○ Other Company's Station

Luton Leagrave

St Albans

TRACKS

Single

Multiple

Multiple Electrified
25 kV AC Overhead
Line Equipment

Single

St Pancras - - - - →

Figure 134. Leicestershire, Rutland, Lincolnshire, Northamptonshire, Bedfordshire and London.

The last journey heads south for London but also takes in the Midland Railway line from Syston in Leicestershire to Peterborough to connect with the Great Northern and the East Coast Main Line.

Loughborough

Date Built	Railway/Design	Platforms	Passengers 2016–2017	Listed
1872	Midland Railway	3	1.317 million	Grade II

Loughborough has a long association with railway engineering and the Brush Traction works is located just outside the station. The Great Central station is extant with the Great Central heritage railway.

Loughborough station is 111 miles and 46 chains (180 km) from St Pancras via Leicester.

Above: Figure 135. The station building at Loughborough is, according to the Historic England listing, 'of white brick with red brick dressings and hipped slate roofs'. November 2017.

Right: Figure 136. The original booking office at Loughborough has been adapted for modern use and is part of the HE listing. November 2017.

Figure 137. The platform elevations at Loughborough retain enough of their Midland Railway character to rate a mention in the listing. November 2017.

The journey now heads east towards Cambridgeshire and Peterborough.

Melton Mowbray

Date Built	Railway/Design	Platforms	Passengers 2016–2017	Listed
1848	Midland Railway	2	0.265 million	No

Melton Mowbray and other stations on the line exist in a time warp, with some semaphore signalling and largely original stations.

Melton Mowbray station is 105 miles and 22 chains (169 km) from St Pancras via Corby.

Figure 138. Melton Mowbray had been a junction station with a line from Nottingham. The Asfordby branch now leads to the Alstom test centre. November 2017.

Figure 139. A compact but pleasing layout at Melton Mowbray, looking west from the MR footbridge. November 2017.

Figure 140. The signal box is a later LMS production; the line past it leads to Syston Junction and the Asfordby branch leads off to the right some way up the line. November 2017.

Figure 141. The fine detail and quality of the restoration at Melton Mowbray would leave the impression that the building was listed. November 2017.

Oakham

Date Built	Railway/Design	Platforms	Passengers 2016–2017	Listed
1848	Midland Railway	2	0.221 million	Grade II

Into England's smallest county of Rutland and a scene with plenty of MR features, including the signal box, which has been immortalised as the prototype for the Airfix/Dapol model railway kit.

Oakham station is 93 miles and 61 chains (151 km) from St Pancras via Corby.

Above: Figure 142. The main station building at Oakham on Platform 1 is listed, together with the signal box and footbridge. November 2017.

Left: Figure 143. The Airfix kit signal box at Oakham is bearing up well, although the fire buckets would have been on the side wall under the steps in MR service. November 2017.

Figure 144. The MR goods shed stands opposite Platform 2, where the camera is, while a GB Railfreight Class 66, No. 66729, waits in the Up goods loop for the semaphore to come off so it can proceed to Manton Junction with a train of containers. November 2017.

Figure 145. CrossCountry Trains Class 170 No. 170636 disgorges its passengers onto Platform 1. November 2017.

Stamford

Date Built	Railway/Design	Platforms	Passengers 2016–2017	Listed
1848	Midland Railway Sancton Wood	2 (3 faces)	0.356 million	Grade II (part)

Into Lincolnshire now and Stamford Town, to distinguish it from the Great Northern's Stamford East, was influenced by the nearby Burghley House.

The place from which mileages are calculated changes and Stamford station is 10 miles and 11 chains (151 km) from Manton Junction.

Figure 146. The style of architecture at Stamford is described by Historic England as Victorian Gothic. The canopy is unique. The building nearest the camera was a residence. Note the small steps to aid staff climbing onto the platform. July 2006.

Figure 147. Platform 2 at Stamford clearly had a partner platform on the island and the wooden waiting shelter bears testament to this. Neither the waiting shelter nor footbridge is mentioned in the listing. July 2006.

Figure 148. There are no more semaphores to signal at Stamford any longer but the 1893 MR signal box lives on and had been a store for a local bookseller. July 2006.

The journey now reverts to the Midland Main Line at Leicester Midland.

Leicester

Date Built	Railway/Design	Platforms	Passengers 2016–2017	Listed
1894 Rebuilt	Midland Railway Charles Trubshaw	4	5.423 million	Grade II (part)

Leicester has no recognisable MR features on the platforms, so most of the coverage is concerned with the main station building.

Leicester Midland station is 99 miles and 7 chains (159 km) from St Pancras.

Figure 149. Historic England have this to say about Leicester Midland station: 'The porte-cochère is a distinguished example of late C19 railway architecture completed in 1892 by one of the most important and ambitious companies of the era of railway development in England.' The porte-cochère, or covered carriage porch, at Leicester occupies a good deal of the side of the building, with separate arrivals and departures gates. November 2017.

Figure 150. The departure gates at Leicester Midland are divided into 'IN' and 'OUT', as the carved stone inscriptions below the word 'DEPARTURE' tell us. These gates are now for pedestrian access. MR wrought iron gates also feature. November 2017.

Figure 151. Midland Railway finery is seen in the wrought iron gate-work, using 'MR' as a logo. November 2017.

Figure 152. Inside the porte-cochère at Leicester Midland with vehicles admitted at the end and exiting through the far 'ARRIVALS' gate on the right. November 2017.

Figure 153. The passenger concourse at Leicester Midland is decorated with these glazed bricks or tiles. November 2017.

Figure 154. An unusual part of Leicester station is this loco yard with a Class 47, 56 and 58 in attendance, together with departmental coaching and MU stock. November 2017.

Market Harborough

Date Built	Railway/Design	Platforms	Passengers 2016–2017	Listed
1885 Rebuilt	Midland Railway John Livock	2	0.888 million	Grade II (part)

Market Harborough was originally a joint line with the London & North Western Railway, and they and the MR were to meet again further south at Bedford, although at separate stations.

Market Harborough station is 82 miles and 74 chains (133 km) from St Pancras.

Figure 155. Market Harborough is unique among surviving MR stations and could be described as being built in the classical Georgian revival style. October 2006.

Figure 156. Market Harborough station building is below platform level and this covered walkway transports passengers to and from the platform. October 2006.

Figure 157. Market Harborough's goods shed still exists as of the earlier survey date. October 2006.

Kettering

Date Built	Railway/Design	Platforms	Passengers 2016–2017	Listed
1879	Midland Railway	4	1.062 million	Grade II
1898	Attributed		Charles Trubshaw	

Into Northamptonshire now and Kettering services passenger trains from Corby.

Kettering station is 72 miles and 1 chain (116 km) from St Pancras. There is a 72-mile marker post on Platform 1 at Kettering station.

Figure 158. Kettering's boot and shoe trade almost dried up before the Midland Railway arrived and provided new markets. The gable on the left-hand side has the MR initials firmly emblazoned on it. December 2017.

Figure 159. East Midlands Trains Class 222 No. 222014 has arrived at Platform 2 at Kettering from Corby and is headed for St Pancras. December 2017.

Figure 160. Some glazing remains on the canopy of Platform 1 at Kettering, while others have been covered with sheeting. December 2017.

Figure 161. Platforms 2 (nearer) and 3 on the island at Kettering retain the original wooden station building, which is now over 120 years old. The ornate ironwork supporting the saw-tooth canopy has lost its end gabling. December 2017.

Figure 162. Platform 3 on the island at Kettering has been more fortunate and retains the gabling decoration on the canopy. December 2017.

Wellingborough

Date Built	Railway/Design	Platforms	Passengers 2016–2017	Listed
1857 1894	Midland Railway Charles H. Driver	3 (4 Faces)	0.990 million	Grade II

Wellingborough originally had four platforms, with Platform 4 being used for the Higham Ferrers branch trains. However, the fourth was removed sometime in the 1980s.

Wellingborough station is 65 miles and 11 chains (105 km) from St Pancras.

Figure 163. The wooden decorative bargeboards at Wellingborough are standard Victorian fare, but the cross-banded decoration above the windows and doors is a celebration of the wealth of the Midland Railway. December 2017.

Figure 164. The general layout at Wellingborough, looking towards Bedford and St Pancras. The remains of Platform 4 can just be seen on the left. December 2017.

Figure 165. On platforms 2 and 3 the island station building is considerably later than the main at 1894. December 2017.

Above: Figure 166. The listed goods shed at Wellingborough shows cast iron window frames as well as cross-banded brick and stonework. December 2017.

Left: Figure 167. The goods shed crane is a typical example of about a 1½-ton capacity and would lift goods in and out of railway wagons or onto a horse and cart, and latterly a motor lorry. December 2017.

Flitwick

Date Built	Railway/Design	Platforms	Passengers 2016–2017	Listed
1870	Midland Railway	4	1.518 million	No

Into Bedfordshire commuter-land and Flitwick also serves Ampthill.

Flitwick station is 40 miles and 18 chains (65 km) from St Pancras.

Harlington, the next station after Flitwick, has similar Midland Railway buildings but was not included on the survey.

Figure 168. The Midland Railway decided to go to London and in 1870 they built this station at Flitwick on their way. December 2017.

Figure 169. The full panoply of London commuter-land is on view at Flitwick with an EMU and 25 kV OHLE. December 2017.

Luton Leagrave

Date Built	Railway/Design	Platforms	Passengers 2016–2017	Listed
1870	Midland Railway	4	1.862 million	No

After Luton the line enters Hertfordshire through St Albans, which has a preserved MR signal box, and then finally reaches London.

Luton Leagrave station is 32 miles and 30 chains (52 km) from St Pancras.

Figure 170. The stationmaster's residence at the far end of the building at Luton Leagrave has a bay window, from which proper station working could be observed, on or off duty. December 2017.

St Pancras

Date Built	Railway/Design	Platforms	Passengers 2016–2017	Listed
1868	Midland Railway William H. Barlow	15	38.076 million	Grade I (part)

The former poet laureate John Betjeman is credited with saving St Pancras after the destruction of the LNWR's Doric arch at Euston in the 1960s.

Mileages are started from St Pancras, so the buffer stops here are the zero datum point.

Figure 171. The Midland Railway was a latecomer to London, so some statement as to power and wealth had to be made. November 2017.

Figure 172. Looking across the frontage and main entrance at St Pancras to the former Midland Grand Hotel at the far end. Historic England describe the outside as '... deep red Gripper's patent Nottingham bricks with Ancaster stone dressings and shafts of grey and red Peterhead granite.' This was the first station to be built of something other than London bricks, as they could be transported in by train. November 2017.

Above: Figure 173. With the clock tower on the near left, Pancras Road runs along the east side of the station. Across the road, to the right, is the Great Northern Hotel and King's Cross station. November 2017.

Right: Figure 174. Once a demolition prospect, George Gilbert Scott's hotel is once more a byword for luxury and comfort. November 2017.

Figure 175. Inside, Barlow's MR train shed roof still dominates the scene with the international platforms on the left, which are elevated, screened off from the station ground floor. The *Meeting Place* sculpture is a 2008 addition by Paul Day. November 2017.

Figure 176. John Betjeman has been immortalised by Martin Jennings in this 2007 sculpture. The Butterley Iron Company's 1867 steelwork holds up the roof. November 2017.

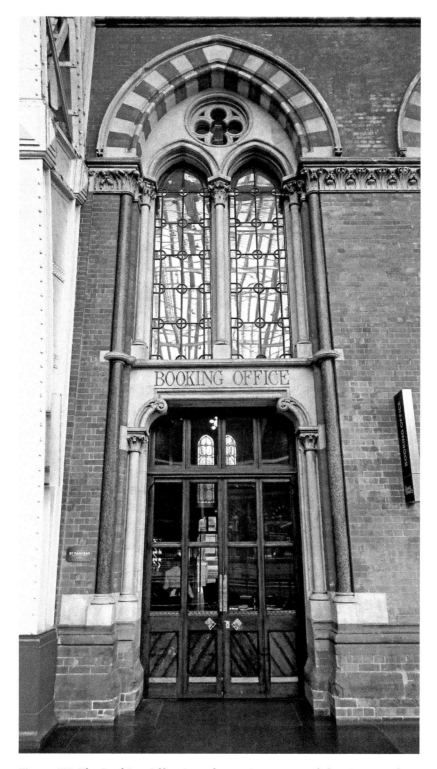

Figure 177. The Booking Office is no longer in use as such but is a temple to grandeur and magnificence. November 2017.

Figure 178. The Midland Road entrance could also be mistaken for a cathedral. November 2017.

A postscript now follows in the form of Cheltenham Spa, which has no other stations with MR buildings nearby and so cannot constitute a journey. There is a signal box at Alstone Crossing nearby, which was covered in a previous volume.

Gloucestershire

Cheltenham Spa

Date Built	Railway/Design	Platforms	Passengers 2016–2017	Listed
1840	Midland Railway Samuel Daukes	2	2.544 million	No

Cheltenham Spa Lansdown is one of several stations that have existed in the town, but this is the only survivor.

Cheltenham Spa station is 86 miles and 58 chains (140 km) from Derby London Road Junction.

Figure 179. Cheltenham Spa is quite unlike any other MR station but has a Midland Hotel like so many others. February 2018.

Figure 180. The station interior style is also quite different, with no saw-tooth canopies, but there is an MR footbridge. The view is towards Birmingham. September 2006.

References and Acknowledgements

Acknowledgements

The kindness and interest shown by railway staff.

References

Books and Printed Works

Bridge, Mike (ed.), *TrackAtlas of Mainland Britain* (Platform 5 Books).

Conolly, Philip W., *British Railways Pre-Grouping Atlas and Gazetteer* (Ian Allan).

Gilkes, John Spencer, *The Nostalgia of Steam Classic Images* (The Nostalgia Collection).

Jackson, Allen, *A Contemporary Perspective of LMS Railway Signalling* Volume 1 (Crowood Publishers).

Quail Track Diagrams Parts 2 and 4 (TrackMaps).

Internet Web Sites

Google Maps

https://historicengland.org.uk/listing/the-list/

https://www.visitnorthwest.com/sights/settle-carlisle-railway/